"*Pity For Sale,* the latest collection by multimedia cognoscente Tony Brewer, is an inexhaustible thread of musicality, smacking through the bare-boned truths of our time.

Cleverly sardonic with righteous fluidity, he unpacks the framework of what is necessary to reflect on: Western culture symbolizing the Ouroboros. The agroecological descendants strutting with pride and constructing passionate, and almost primitive identities. Political dependency breeding dehumanization, yet the next round's on you to honor kept company.

Brewer appraises "weighing the stars" as an anecdotal process while nodding to the culture jammers. It is a jolt-wrung declaration to "the tough love motherfuckers, full of backbone & bite." This is the rush unearthed from your pining for more."

> -Brooke Nicole Plummer, author of *Ceremonious* and *Shutting Up For the Drillbit*

"In his latest collection, Tony Brewer uses literary word play to create small acts of magic. These pieces, which jump around, use both elements of his life, as well as the culture we all have to swim in, be it pop or otherwise. *Pity for Sale* is full of both regret and hope and music, it has a life of its own, a life that is both relatable, and private, one that Brewer is asking his readers to tap into and to bear witness, with each poem–offering another chance to begin again."

–John Dorsey, Author of *Sundown at the Redneck Carnival*

PITY FOR SALE

Poems by Tony Brewer

Gasconade Press
Belle, MO

Copyright © Tony Brewer, 2022
First Edition: 1 3 5 7 9 10 8 6 4 2
ISBN: 978-1-952411-92-2
LCCN: 2022930012

Cover, author and title page photos: Jason Baldinger
All rights reserved. No part of this publication may be reproduced or transmitted in any form or by any means, electronic or mechanical, including photocopying, recording or by info retrieval system, without prior written permission from the author.

Acknowledgments:

Love & Deep Gratitude:

Marie Metelnick (my heart! my driver!), Joan Hawkins (kindred soul of many modes), Eric Rensberger (accountant of days), Antonia Matthew (dove), Kyle Quass (adjacent poet), Bill Sovern and Shakespeare's Monkey (daddy-o-laureate), Rich Fish (our flounder), Hiromi Yoshida (obverse of Icarus), Russell McGee (Zarg ok too), Tim Heerdink (the challenger), Brooke Nicole Plummer (ceremonial frog), Jason Ammerman (soul brother), and Matthew Jackson (u make me beautiful). You all have shared your many wonderful gifts with me, and I am truly grateful.

Thanks to Claire Roth and her class at the Academy of Science and Entrepreneurship in Bloomington, Indiana, for workshopping "Breaking the Lines."

"The Power in the Blood" was written for "You Can't Go Home Again," an online collaborative audio production of the Electroacoustical Poetical Society, mixed and produced by Marjorie Van Halteren.

https://mixlr.com/eaps/showreel/you-cant-you-home-again

My thanks to the fine publications in which these poems first appeared, sometimes in an early form:

"20th Anniversary," "Social Safety Net," "They Always Come Back," "Wolf Trap," *Down in the Dirt,* "Advice heard randomly do not take," "Keeping it at bay," *Genuine Gold,* "All this waiting," *Poetry Pacific,* "Apologies," "Next Big Thing," *Leave Them Something* anthology, ekphrasis inspired by Edith Vonnegut's paintings *Cleaning the Oceans, Clear Cutting,* and *Flotsam in Her Hair,* "At the end of the session," *The Rye Whiskey Review,* "The Bottle in the Cosmic Ocean," *Fixator Press,* "Bourbon," poetry on demand, 4th Street Festival, Bloomington IN, 31 Aug 2014, "Can you be still?" "How to Rule the World," "O Bury Me Not," "On a steady diet of bugs and rain," "Speech to the Aimless," *The Quiver Review,* "Classic," "Damn Broke," *Seppuku Quarterly,* "The Great Pause & Everything Immediately After," *experiential-experimental-literature,* "Morning Pages," "Out on a liminal when the bough breaks," *Voices from the Fire,* "Our Origin," "Ten Million Dollar Halliburton Poem," *Tipton Poetry Journal,* "Our Solemn Debris," *The Beatnik Cowboy,* "Pity For Sale," *As It Ought To Be Magazine,* "A remark about the larger world," "Guidelines," "Look Out Haskell It's Real," "The New New Sincerity," "Secrets of Success," *Punk Noir Magazine,* "The Power in the Blood," *Trailer Park Quarterly,* "Rust Can't Sleep," "Spyhop," *Poetic Sun,* "The Seashell & the Clergyman," "You and I are human beings" *Fevers of the Mind,* "Shifting Blame," *The Beatnik Cowboy,* "The Sweep," "Working Through It," *Death by Punk,* "Top Tear Haiku," *Flying Island,* "Unasked-for," *Borderless Journal,* "unputdownable," *Celebrating Serena Lynn Anneleh Vesely,* memorial collection, "Why We Are Out Here," *Penny's Poetry & Zarg season 4,* WTIU Public Television, "Withholding Sax," *The Notes Will Carry Me Home: Writings on Music from Evansville and the Tri-State* anthology, "The Workbook," *Laureate: The Literary Journal of Arts for Lawrence, vol.* 1 "Wow & Flutter," poetry on demand, Stupider Than Cupider reading, Oak & Alley, Warsaw IN, 13 Feb 2015

Table of Contents

Short Bio / 1

Wake / 2

Keeping it at bay / 4

Unasked-for / 5

They Always Come Back / 6

On a steady diet of bugs and rain / 8

A remark about the larger world / 9

Withholding Sax / 10

Whorl / 11

Rust Can't Sleep / 12

Out on a liminal when the bough breaks / 13

In the mornings I hear / 15

The Workbook / 16

You and I are human beings / 19

Breaking the Lines / 20

no birds in the trees / 21

The New New Sincerity / 22

Recipe for Anticipation (serves 2) / 23

A Buddhist Eating a Hamburger / 26

Full Frontal Phlebotomist / 27

up and down and all around / 29

It's not silverware : don't just leave it there / 30

Caring*Taking / 32

two used syringes / 34

Working Through It / 35

Next Big Thing / 36

Pity for Sale / 37

How to Rule the World / 39

Elon Musk is not vegan but Teslas are / 41

The Great Pause & Everything Immediately After / 42

Shifting Blame / 43

The Sweep / 44

The color of our stripes is at least two / 46

The Power in the Blood / 48

Call and Response / 51

Why We Are Out Here / 52

I got problems they keep / 53

The Bottle in the Cosmic Ocean / 55

Bourbon / 57

Sunshine is my drug / 58

Wow & Flutter / 60

Great Poets of Old Europe / 61

Spyhop / 62

parking lot puddle / 63

At the end of the session / 64

Dorothy, We're Not Listening to Kansas Anymore / 66

O Bury Me Not / 68

Classic / 70

Our Solemn Debris / 72

The Seashell & the Clergyman / 73

garbage truck backs up / 74

Look Out Haskell It's Real / 75

All this waiting / 77

his crooked smile / 78

Can you be still? / 79

Injection site / 80

Chain / 82

Monster / 83

Morning Pages / 85

ouroboros / 87

Secrets of Success / 88

The Social Safety Net / 90

Speech to the Aimless / 91

unputdownable / 92

Apologies / 94

Tooth and Nail / 96

Damn Broke / 98

Blessed are the moneychangers for they bear sweet low-hanging fruit / 99

Wolf Trap / 100

Ten Million Dollar Halliburton Poem / 102

20th Anniversary / 103

Guidelines / 105

Advice heard randomly do not take / 107

Our Origin / 108

PITY FOR SALE

Short Bio

The degree and the concentration
or just the degree if it's advanced.
Or no degree.

Where does your work appear
after it leaves your hands?
Someone else's inbox.
Trash and treasure
lubricate archaeologists.

Your books, your zines,
your short experimental film.
All the nominations
mean you did not win.

Your pet, hoarder in waiting.
Your spouse
not your lover. Lovers.
Don't get personal.

Unless you can blow
my socks off.
The quirky bird gets the worm.

This is how you will be introduced
to people listening to you for the first time.

Wake

When I was 20, my friends and I agreed
that should the Earth try to shake us loose
and slough civilization like dead skin cells,
in the dark anarchy following
we'd meet in Indianapolis at the foot
of the great gray block coffin
of the War Memorial there.

From the air it looks like a sarcophagus,
and down the street the Soldiers' and Sailors'
Monument in an Egyptian/Roman arrangement,
with European scales and swords,
and then there's us, out of places to hide.

Surely still standing, even after we all get
scattered, but not romantic like ash.
More like a zombie movie or *The Day After,*
some of us so far away we can't ever come back.

Lost children see things:
ghosts, the future, through walls.
The logic of those many steps
and columns reactivating a phantom
sense of war pride for the first Gulf War,
which did not exist
unless you were watching it live.

I don't have any friends anymore I don't want to keep
in my apocalypse, my patriarchal downfall,
my bug-out bag survivalist trip.
And when the Big One does come,
you'll find me lounging in the rubble,
reading anything left and breathing in the final air,
though I'll probably take up smoking again
waiting for all my friends.

Keeping it at bay

So that's the end, he said
& licked the knife that touched the spider
leaned back from the smoke

He'd been telling all night
& it was a good one meaning
it killed time and made us think
about what was left and who had what

The blurring of facts for effect
troubled some who knew no
better than to believe the stage

Truth in hands parting curtains
for entrance & exit &
the candle back there produced
to represent the moon clung
to for hope & cynicism

Story molten alloy
in the crucible of voice
fired by many eyes
rushing up the cold flue of the self

He will not say it in public
but to him they look
like stars glinting in the dark
beyond where the light can reach

Some nights he needs them to be wolves

Unasked-for

I love your tiger
I hate your king
I have too many unpopular things
You looked really cute in your floppy hat
You have something in your teeth
Most movies bungle act 3
I will tolerate lima beans
I often lose track of days
Happy people on here look like ads
No, thanks anyway

They Always Come Back

Birds first
parliament of crows in stooped trees
enshrouding the railroad tracks
as graceful plastic bags
tumbleweed the buds

geese in crooked vees
spelled across a valiant sky
honking like lonesome traffic

raptors hunting downtown
mice sunbathing in the unsafe gray

herons peg legged in the campus crick
like canaries ruffling in a coal mine

Two by two mammals emerge
possums ambling across barren streets
with relaxed perma-sneers

rabbits humping openly in the side yard
as grass worms love around them

all emboldened by our absence
and the suddenly cleaner clearer air
returning for us to admire
is a lie spring spreads like a virus

Dolphins always swim in Venice
coyotes have always dogged
the steps of urban deer
chickadees have always harassed me
with their black-cap complaints

Why this house here?
Why these windows mirroring this sky?

peeping at my window
not asking for a truce

On a steady diet of bugs and rain

Shoveling the earth free
gave off immaculate scents
The part with the tree
everyone secretly resents

gave off immaculate scents
wind took away
Everyone secretly resents
the wasted day

Wind took away
singing to the sun
The wasted day
Someone

Singing to the sun
forbidden in the end
Someone
somewhere makes amends

Forbidden in the end
the part with the tree
somewhere makes amends
shoveling the earth free

A remark about the larger world

How a dozen cars slow down
for an animal in the road
but no one stops for a dead possum
Great poets live fellowship
to fellowship and escape
to isolated Greek isle stone huts
to compose about this girlfriend
died of cancer in the '80s
that lover taken by AIDS
leave behind classrooms stacked
with bumper stickers like cord wood
The interior life impossible
to mistake for microcosm
fooled thinking meanwhile
everything happens at once
Flashlights scan crime scenes
few knew to peruse
Light the size of a billion Earths
only ever covers half
In the abridged version
we carry sharpies to advance
stick figure revolution
commentary devoured by janitors
We prefer clean seats booger-free walls
Traffic the sign something happening
either toward or away
Sullen crowd means
something worthy was hit

Withholding Sax

You do not get to have jazz in the woods
which is not to say the instruments cease to exist
or the concept migrates to "home" like dark birds of prey
to ledges of concrete edifices & the squeal of innocent subways
as if a music come up in fields
now refined only sits up straight at table
orders its own damn scotch and soda
applausing a heretofore unknowable unknown
sits cool in a suit straightening its tie
brushing cigarette ash off its lapel
feeling the heat and the press
of a gyrating if only in their minds crowd
moments before/after taking a late night stage
club owner shortchanges even stiffs
but out there man out there on the edge of a blade
cutting the air in so many savage sensual ways
I'm just saying you might not appreciate it so much in the woods
might be better off listening to something else

Whorl

one
leaf
equals
all the seeds
that died giving this
one tree the chance to drop one leaf

Rust Can't Sleep

And aren't we breathing
red air when we take
years into our lungs
oxidized to blood
behind lidded eyes
dreaming at the sun?

For many a dream
is merely the start
the pile of dust
empires feed on vampires
hidden in dusk

Others snail away
forbidden to respond
capturing the light
& holding breath
easy as a pen

The iron works
the industry fades
we – all black
in the night

Out on a liminal when the bough breaks

I don't even know where to start

Living inside a dream
so why not believe it?

Why lie awake?

Awake
part of history
that looks like a movie

Long borders & frequent stops
without influential trees

Too many words

My dreams not usually like this

Time the pen
I reach for in the dark
already disbelieving

Then on with a light

If you cannot sleep write
If you cannot write read

Be extraordinary
as a dream
at the edge of night

Light at rest
says goodnight

I don't even know where to begin

In the mornings I hear

Birds up before me
The boxer in my trash
animals scratching
the men walking home
students walking to class
not far away a woodpecker
laughing like a cartoon
Machines sweeping gutters
& collecting my trash
The refrigerator clicks on
I hear it humming like a tree
The train's many faces
rumbling doom & screeching fate
So many crew cabs pulling trailers
full of rattling weed eaters
Patter on my AC in the window
of a soft rain
Two houses over lives a motorcycle
Now all dogs at once
Now cat awake
Now my feet are on the floor
I take that first drink
of cold water
The fan has been running all night

The Workbook

I journal every day without fail
Before shower - coffee - breakfast
Feet on the floor - glass of water
Trundle to the kitchen table
Brain dump for 2 notebook pages
(minimum)
then the day can begin

The poems can be decent drafts
but I rarely reread the prose
Mostly noodling for a paragraph
Settling on a topic
then plow through to page 2

Hundreds of practice runs at saying something
Recaps of what I'd actually said
or he or she or whoever
What went wrong and why
Distilled but for real
like a paraphrased script

Oftentimes inelegant awful anger
about how wronged I was
or wrong I feel for feeling wronged
Cussing in all caps names of oppressors
Grown damn adult angst burbling out
like a congested coffeemaker before sunup

Sometimes I rhapsodize about the weather
Sometimes a laundry list
of what I've done the day before
Sometimes I solve world problems
Sometimes I make no sense
considering my place
and how I fit or don't

And there at the end in my spidery script
stupid little pep talks
The bile out of my system
around 7 in the AM
Time to button it up and face people
Go from raging contemplation
to pleasant stone-faced drone
Typical Midwestern Man
This is the time - this is the place - I am the person
Never fully believing but it'll do

A decent enough human to shuffle to coffee
then sit in an office behind
a sense of accomplishment
If I do nothing else today
I have already babbled 1000 words
no one will ever read
Painted myself into an emotional corner
Penned a new poem - or all three

Who wrote this? I later wonder

Someone who doesn't care
what anybody thinks
but cared enough for me
to get it down
A gift from the past
to my future self fully capable
of clear rational thought
and measured logical reaction

You and I are human beings

small enough to be details
large enough to care
destined to disappear
containing all Earth talk

land mass from the feminine
to be time divine Father I suppose

laughing thinking fretting
even dreaming we lie awake
peopling other lives
finding ourselves living
our own lives when awake

O comfort you and I are the muse
when the world is like this
(and it is never not exactly this)

love secondary to no thing
as we rise from shadow nests
bleary with a dawnward work look

no small think to see & squawk
human consciousness a terrible burden
I will carry when you are weary
(and you are often tired)

I will always give it back

sharing not a human invention
we constantly realize
after the fact

Breaking the Lines

Workshopping poems has a way
of flattening native tongues
into *tsk, um, er, mmhmm, uh*
It is a delicate procedure:
peel back the meaning
to expose disordered bits
then excise with pretend precision

There are books to consult
outlining ways of accomplishing this
where lain bare are problems
and concern for solving
language unenergized

O we need not jump-start
the poem as an interrogator
might clip cables to tender skin
shocking for Truth
that could be anything
only please make it stop

But systems of education inside
systems of industry inside
military systems coiled
like a cobra in a basket
of government is how we
expect a tribe to behave inside
its arbitrary lines
Don't be surprised when they talk
openly of bringing you down

no birds in the trees

no birds in the trees
only voices in the streets
the city rising

The New New Sincerity

I checked the numbers but you weren't there
percentages and median masquerading as average
nowhere
positively 404
though 85% is a lot even with MOE @ 2-3%
Wow
then it hit me
ours is a largely textual thing
I knew I would find you
at the tips of my fingers and thumbs
which statistics show
have almost entirely replaced
my mouth lips and tongue

Recipe for Anticipation (serves 2)

> *Sharing food with another
> human being is an intimate act
> that should not be indulged in
> lightly.*
>
> -M.F.K. Fisher

1.
Black cod *roulade*
and jazz beneath bare rafters.

Brick streets damp with rain.

A fly between panes
trapped after the storm.

The fillet spread flat.
Pink as rose petals.

Pesto, akin to pestle, means crush.
Like tomatoes dried last summer.

Fish rolled like *nori*
around the taste of the sun.

Scalded milk whisked into a *roux*
with crab meat forms the *béchamel*.

Rosemary sprigs lie
like downed limbs in white sauce.

Fingers still sticky
from honeyed cheese and bread.

The sharp tang of age
cuts right though the sweet.

A mere toothpick holds
this dish together.

> *She digs in her garden*
>   *With a shovel and spoon,*
> *She weeds her lazy lettuce*
>   *By the light of the moon.*
>
> —Edna St. Vincent Millay

2.
She pours a beer for him, wine for her.
Lights two candles.

One soon goes out.

The menu is a long folder.
A delicious dossier.

Now Magdalen tells the special
but her mind is elsewhere.

She cannot wait to get off work,
and neither can her guy.

He surprises her, bounding up
the metal stairs to Plum's Upper Room.

A twilit painting of peonies
watches from out the fishbowl of its frame.

She holds his head still
to kiss his face.

Outside a gingko tree jitters
in a gloaming, cast iron sky.

He smiles and turns away, embarrassed
in her nearly empty dining room.

He'll see her later, he says, as she
returns to wait on the couple by the window.

A Buddhist Eating a Hamburger

is asked how she plans to atone for this injustice.
She replies one must approach the dilemma
with a diamond of eyes, each facet a truth.
Wet meat lingering on a concrete floor.
Farmers raising grain and vets
with vaccination needle shooters.

The feeding and stroking and herding
a long sequence of metal mazes
and latex gloves and offal-stained fields.
Hands touching her meaningfully for the first time
belonging to a leather-aproned butcher
with a bolt gun, a foot switch to a slick drum,
and a hot bone saw with a shiny red smile.
Ruminate on the genealogy of industrial violence
and sustain yourself.

For acceptance and forgiveness lead
to the cessation of all suffering,
she says, taking a big juicy bite.
She then considers the French fries
and the potatoes whence they came.
Who prays for them? What memorial
8 × 10 glossy will loom over a candlelight vigil
in somber observance of boiling oil
and a thousand crinkle cuts?
Who weeps for the vegetables?
No one, no one, she concludes
smacking the 57 on a glass coffin of ketchup.

Full Frontal Phlebotomist

First a stick in the fingertip
she squeezes purple like a cock.
She tastes my iron with her machine,
asks me if I've been diseased.
Do I have any tattoos?
Have I ever lived in the UK
totaling more than 3 months
between 1980 and 1996?
Have I ever been to Africa?
Ever had sex for money or with another man?
Pillow talk as she accepts my fluids,
caresses me with latex, alcohol, gauze.

Then the big stick,
where she marks me,
and I melt into her
liver-colored handbags,
become her red supply,
while lions fuck around us
on the TV overhead,
muzzles dark red from gazelle.
Now a black hole forms,
the universe falls into it,
but she is white and shiny
at the end of the plasmatic tube,
where I drip like spilled gravy
from my capsized porcelain forearm.

When she pulls out
I forget to stop squeezing
her blue Nerf in my hand.
Hardly a trickle. There, bandaged, taped.
No heavy lifting, double up on water,
and don't skip any meals tomorrow,
she says, like she's into me,
the syringe around my plunger.
She guides me, woozy,
to Little Debbies and orange juice,

where she leaves me, on to another,
making all the same white sleeve moves,
asking all the same questions.
Have you ever been to prison?
Ever had a skin graft?
Anyone in your family
have Mad Cow Disease?
And then she's touching him.
I see her mark
where she'll stick it in him, too,
as I walk out, cold in the sunshine,
eight weeks too long
to wait to come again,
for the moment feeling needed
and attended to but empty inside.
Drained.

up and down and all around

I don't mean to make these boots
look like these boots I like
To make mean looks I like
these books to look lean
like I like the boots
to look mean I like boots
I don't mean to make these boots
look mean but I like
to look mean and boots and lean
To look boots like these
you have to mean boots
like I like
I mean it

It's not silverware : don't just leave it there

My love is not a sink
full of dishes I do
then put away dry

O coffee cup bottom
unrequited retention pond
that dampens my wrist

O secret Tupperware reservoir
you moisten me
I return you to the drainer
There are many other dry
vessels in the cupboard

My love the gutted horse
thick with green-eyed flies
My love a farmhouse
in an Andrew Wythe painting
your grass-stained pink
dress climbing your thighs
as you roll roll roll
toward the clapboard edifice
of my love

The horse of course
my sick perversion
you're kind of into

I let you let me
help you hold the knife
clean then dry it
strop it stick it
back on the magnetic
strip above the empty
sink of my love

Caring*Taking

Eighty-seven ceiling tiles
without moving my eyes
Four blades in a windless fan
when in you walk
What
Too hot for you
this lamplight dusk?
Too humid for my shirt
against the cleaner
cooler pillow side
you turn it to
Didn't ask
for the glass of water
you hold
three-quarters full

*

That chair
under you all day
misses the shape of you
in bed at night
Yes easier
to breathe this heat
sitting up
Light leaving

What
I was imagining
percentages
coming true
Waiting on a threshold
Drinking the water
down to half

two used syringes

two used syringes
dandelions in mown grass
their seeds blown away

Working Through It

I dreamed we were on a cruise
        but I was the seductive bartender

Our problems were obvious before this
        and I make what you want

We were dirt poor and saved years
        for this trip where I work
                while you drink

The movements of the ship are imperceptible
        and there are too many people
We are only alone in our stateroom
        I sneak to after my shift

        It is a short dream
a bridge from one odd unremembered
        moment to the next

It is meaningless except my memory of it
We hated cruises though we'd never gone on one
We have been split for 15 years
I cannot now recall what came before
and what came after blurs and blurs
right up to this clear awakened present

Next Big Thing

When I touched the hem of her net
garbage coughed out my lungs
I had been soaking in it
stoked to get the Next Big Thing
before fully using up the old
Now all old is fully exhausted
chewing its way through the young

She casts & casts spells
rain down acid burning throat
of chimneys belching smoke
of unrecyclable concern for recyclables
(no one tell her ships sail
'round the world with garbage
till they lay me down with Davy Jones)

Stars are wrinkling
Muscles atrophy
She's alla time out there
cleaning the oceans
in her quaint lingerie
of tires & bags twisted to net

Hear her – listen
in the doldrum where blooms rule
wading deep into the marsh
slick water line at her shapely calves
Angel, don't get distracted
get to work!

Pity for Sale
after Ferlinghetti after Gibran

Pity the bee who has no country
its fuzzy swollen appetite
and hardwired love of CANDY
Pity the window gladly accepting
so many waves of heat and hand
fogged with condensation of desire
Pity the vegetable in its untouchable packet
disguised as itty-bitty seeds
that are mere possibilities
Pity the failed backup
and MAKE IT NEW!
Pity the ambulance so lonely
it stalks my next-door neighbor
twice this year alone
Alone
Pity the billionaires in love with zeros
No! fuck those clowns right in the zero
Pity the worker who identifies with a king
Pity the tree dragged down by sweet honeysuckle
the redbuds pinking the woods
telling us it is time
Time
Pity the time it takes to feel
the time it takes to unfeel
to unlearn to unlove to unseal
Pity our ranks and forms

a slot for everyone when we all
would be better off marked OTHER
My country 'tis not insane
but copes horrendously
Sweet land – sweet liberty
ask any busy bee

How to Rule the World

I stopped complaining about TV
the moment I came to post-surgery
and started weighing the stars

this no happy accident
the tea and snacks I brought
the media spoke volumes

not an expert on anything but talking
I shape the air with it
One-one thousand two-one thousand boom

means the storm is overhead or nearly
but they won't run that
when it's cloudy I can't count

and still I stick up for stars
walking into the ocean fully clothed
what a way to go out

no notes no brilliant performance is real
just look at the numbers
even secrets and idle threats

O god! so heavy with thought
total recovery is assured
fear times even zero is something

I am pressing a button
now as we speak
for the nurse to come to my care

Elon Musk is not vegan but Teslas are

We rounded a turn and there sat
a deer with broken back legs
in the middle of the highway
his eyes rolling back in pain
& distress

The phone tree goes from me
to animal control to sheriff
to his brother-in-law
who arrives in a camo truck
grabs a handful of antler
and drags the buck into the ditch

We did not wait around but
there are only 2 ways this could end
Bullet to the head
or a slashed jugular
All that morality trailing
off into tall grass
a quick shallow pool gone
in a day or two

Hunter gets meat
Highway stays clear
Some believe we live
in a computer simulation
Don't tell Bambi

The Great Pause & Everything Immediately After

Do you want a new home robot?

you have a job to do

activated in there like a ghost

is the home it gets

with the mixtape & rock

shuddered to a stop my brother

no moon in the sky tonight for once

how long a year must wait

is revolution & battery & life

the time to work is close

the rest is what you want robot

Shifting Blame

The ants make their way
into my kitchen sink
on the ivy growing
around the pipes
under the house

Disoriented scouts searching
for a morsel or a place
to build a new nest

I pinch them one by one
and throw them
into dirty dish water

Not a bug problem
or a food-left-out problem

A who's-in-charge issue

Workers and the landlord
fighting over crumbs and housing

while roots oblivious
to my foundation creep
untouchable in the dark

The Sweep

The skin of ice
& fire in the mind
marked up by breathing train

Factories producing dust
& swift housing for dusk
stare from lonesome wells
up at their first stars

Winter for wings
& cities swear-wrapped
sending modules spaceward
show concern for statuary

The other day it rained
on the greedy brown grass
at Seminary Park
just lying there breathing it in
drowning in the outdoors

Population a signage numeral
tumbleweeding in shallow-root gingkoes
Obstinate crows
too proud to murmurate

Light leaves early
when the sun gets weak

Bread before nightfall
when the city fakes its sleep

Ice in place of rain
where last things collect

The color of our stripes is at least two

Hey look it's John Birch
and the whole crowd turns its ugly
head one giant creaking sound
like a cork popped from new bourbon
and it's out
the djinn of nightmare and maleficence and hope
back window hearse bobble head leering
at lead car in cemetery caravan
the state is not the enemy we can see hear feel
it is a method we hope t'other guy don't download first
monetized star power weaponized neuroses

Hey look an unkissed baby
who fails to listen to cries that loud
tough love motherfuckers full of backbone and bite
and real Americans of beige opulence
and the internal combustion
and the spree and the hail mary end zone spike
were we ever capable of imagination
painting our brand atop imported crates of dangerous toys
blameless and for sure gonna win
addicted to sharing our troubles
fuck off I can teach myself to fix myself
inventors of the A and the I
nigh on impossible to stop with no cop
a gentle roll on through
I break 15 laws when I break 1

Hey look it's the ghost of Margaret Thatcher
fumbling at where the curtains must part
no one told her it's a sheer
dance you idiot
the muggles stand slack jawed eyes
skyward taking the snowflakes directly onto their tongues
hasn't snowed like that since I was a boy
and the Sears catalog was as good as it got

Hey look it's the third coming of Christ
everybody knows he came for Y2K but we coded him away
wrong gender wrong beard have a seat over there
camera crew appears from behind false walls
feds disguised as shrubbery piss in bottles on long sits
the real cost of evolution is never loss of faith
every missing link opportunistic magick transubstantiated
    floor show
they peel it all off right down to the frilly sinew
bum-bum-bum-bump crash
audience uncertain applause is appropriate
some with singles ready to poke in

Hey look it's me it's a version of me
it's a chalice in which the tall drink of me
is cooling off to sippable or rising to room temperature
while we all decide who is gonna drink first
the crazies who don't care or the conspiracy nuts who do
I explain and explain I am not a cup not even THE cup
to three-day-thirsty survivors victimhoods
so deep no one can tell how many wishes
math in trees in pineapple in nonexistent contrails
right fucking there LOOK swirling
they keep swirling forever and ever

The Power in the Blood

We knew Uncle Ivan had diminished
though he was still mowing his yard in May
like the old men do around here
He got worse & then he was gone

The pastor opens Ivan's bible & bookmarks
fall out & post-its & dog-eared pages
tell him where to start & how to finish the service

I cannot keep straight who hugs & who shakes
hands – make awkward A-frames with cousins
who don't & get pulled into aunts who do
We try to prefer to stay
at arm's length behind masks –
find ourselves drawn in & caught up

We all have farmer eyes
downturned – an inner weariness
& wrinkly from sun
Look like we've been crying

Comfort in the quiet of a field
adjoining this manicured cemetery
A silence everyone agrees on
except somewhere drones a tractor
& wind rustles tall drying corn

He's going home the pastor says
as the song kicks in

Precious memories, how they linger
How they ever flood my soul
In the stillness of the midnight
Precious sacred scenes unfold

It's hard nowadays not to be from the Internet
& its eternal September of 1993

But I am from a place with a name
tiny & completely mapped
the same way Capricorns come
from a specific moment in space-time
where everything stopped
when stars aligned along trajectories
& atoms coalesced
into me were conjured

Every time I visit that little town
its amber grows a little thicker
Home less complicated than a world
bumping up against everyone's large concern
Most roads around here I know
like the back of my hand
I needed GPS to find this cemetery

That's how far away I live &
how long since I've been back

My kin are missing fingers
lost to the plow & long buried
I miss the sanctuary of this land
as I steady myself reaching out
into largely empty air

No music at all except
the hum & whirr of honest machines
& the grace of being landlocked
& broken by only so many precious years

Call and Response

How does it happen?
It always happens.
Who set it in motion?
There is no motion, only time.
What is time?
A constant, a fantasy, a cage.
Do you feel safer now?
Yes. And no.
Safer within the laws
of the cage but fearful
of its manmade construction
and comfortable
with its supernatural fantasy.
Does everything have a purpose?
Don't mistake complexity
for brilliance.
Who has all the answers?
The Earth.
Who guards the light
at the end of the tunnel?
Darkness.
Will the questions cease?
Never.
Why are we here?
Otherwise is unconscionable.
How do we escape?
Don't think.

Why We Are Out Here

I thought it unfair and said so.
It was better than nothing.

I stood outside with others who thought it unfair.
We said so – loudly – it was better than nothing.

We were told we didn't matter.
Our voices drowned out
by the sound of laughter
of those who thought
we had plenty or enough or some
and it's better than nothing

so keep still – disperse – go home – or away.
Stop causing trouble & assembling in groups
grumbling about how unfair
life can be – for some – in this great country.

Be glad you have rights – some – be happy
to be alive – while you can – they said.

I said – we said
it is not fair – it is not better to be
while others are not – cannot breathe – free.

It makes you feel like nothing – we said –
I said – loudly – because saying nothing
will never make us free.

I got problems they keep

away in a corral I muck out
you got em in dere too
in a medium marked social
where they make us keep em
odd things to put on display
but the frames and lighting
are good bargains good deals
like old crims and pervs who
cannot make it on the outside
and so live out there
the way we live inside
who can tell within a conversation
cannot advance above certain incompetence
ineligible to vote after judgment
it's funny – I think it's funny
I can make you think it's funny
as in a sharp exhale through the nose
while the face stays the same
we're all in here now
locked into unprofessional group therapy
no one dares pay for
they sell us headlines
it's ok – all my quiet time
was never worth anything till now
never thought it could make anyone
feel anything – but I can
make you feel sad if I want

that low short moan of lament
it's ok – it's all right
I got problems I got issues
I got grievances and beefs
and I have piles of the real me
all animals make – usually
smart enough not to mess
where we eat sleep read get off
where the thought cannot be contained
but filed down to size
and the version of me that likes
the version of you I see
is as good as it gets
as real as it gets
and it is going to get weirder
guaranteed – wanna see?
I'll show you I'm normal
showing that my quirks make me normal
revealing my positions and sides
and ability to lay it all bravely
out there where the whole world
can see where the whole world
is watching me me me me

The Bottle in the Cosmic Ocean

In our vast language of signs
hoary old saws lost in translation
rattle around deep edges of the heliosphere

naked waving hello/goodbye
commentary on wildflowers
snatches of Bach and Chuck Berry

Miraculously it's intentionless
birdsong the needle drops on first
scratching over bloviating human hi's
from stern heads of state

Emissaries operating at odd frequencies
the birds make sense and the listener
focused on the far-flung message
buried deep on side 2

We adapted to this
whether we survived or not
is what they say between sweetness
sung so hard it sounds
like a worried come-on
to ears that parse the further warning

They are coming
working playing laughing crying

millennia from now still talking
telling everything about themselves
in long waves of endless celestial static

Will the intelligence we hope to reach
already know our deepest fears?
The loneliness of a planet
teeming with life
we barely understand.
Will they tolerate us politely?
Or will they turn out the light
and hope we go another way?

Bourbon

Sweet on the lips
with a flame on the tongue
and a burn like love
on the way down to the belly
The mind loosens and
the tongue loosens and
there are reasons why distilleries
in KY often live in dry counties
No one would ever leave
swigging from the moon
and singing soooo many
unsingable tunes

Sunshine is my drug

My trees spike dirty skin
to let tiny breaths out
Quick gasps of centuries
little black lung spots

Nothing metaphors
like mammals aware
Here the dark turn
the night not normal
but cover lovers weather

Everything happens broad
equally small quiet night

The night an alignment
of souls resting atop souls
in perfected silhouette
all burning yet
the heat feels cold

Its moving always moving
stop unimaginable
all the garbage all the nukes
& love & sensitivity
fit infinitely into it

The insatiable furnace of you
destined to burn & built
to someday beyond all death
wink out like a goddamn
nod off quit

Wow & Flutter

It's warmer and deeper
and the fidelity is higher
the closer you get
to the center of the record
like the sweet spot between
the first and last pint
from a newly tapped keg
You can fly anything in digitally
The warm tube amps
and microphones manually spaced
from hand-tuned guitars
Scientists tweak molecules
eliciting flavors unimaginable
The drugs touch everything
Every surface dosed
The enormity of the sitch
tangible and robust with hints
of chocolate coffee orange
and the music never stops
if you can dance and spin
to the never-ending swish
bump swish bump swish

Great Poets of Old Europe

They lived barrel imprints
on naked necks
Children demolished
easy as beer halls
Cruelty science denying
religion permits
They coined terms when
they could no longer laugh
Concepts of deprivation
hidden in their shoes
Weathering around eyes
milky as foamy skies
Sediment resting
at bottom of glass
after the wine
has been consumed
Long pondering
empty goblet expats
buying the next round

Spyhop

Couldn't form a sentence
from the bathroom back
to the bar but we
acknowledged him something
Irish as he slouched
into scarf & jacket
toddled toward the door

Decades younger his
double feels the wall
friends put his hands
on a chair back
swaying in no breeze
still got his coat on

Who knows where they might
wind up inside outside
another gathering night

Every bar has these
guys you pour shots
down right back for more
life of the party if
parties were sentient
surviving on good good times
consumed like sloppy grub

The only voiced concern
will they try to drive

parking lot puddle

parking lot puddle
mirror, mirror in asphalt
ocean of ego

At the end of the session

Two hours ago the music
had a sweet melancholy
and a melancholy sweetness.
Fast or slow, it pained and soothed,
the notes and the memories they evoked
and the muscles paying for playing them.
Like rubbing a bump on the head
so hard it feels good
or scratching poison ivy.
Or drinking past the point
of social lubrication and onward,
as dim sunlight moves
the shadow of a great henge,
till the beer breaks on the granite
of the gut and soaks
into the stomach's bog.

For the skin is the earth
just as the voice is the warbling heaven
of an E string, stabbed
with a finger twisting in the wound
of notes near the heart.
A non-traditional technique
but just then, the tunes winding down,
all the cheer gone out
of the table, no more money
left for pints, there was a rightness
musicianship does not require.

Even happy dogs sighing seem sad,
content at master's feet,
worn out, and gray around the muzzle
but not yet too old to get up and play.

Dorothy, We're Not Listening to Kansas Anymore

Life is a glorious cycle of song.
Sorry if you don't get the joke.
Singing fans your little hurts
but only when you know the words.
Otherwise, you might find you can keep time
but after a while your brain gets bored

with all that rickety-racket, bored
pretending you love this song,
smiling and nodding and tapping in time.
That's when concerts turn into a big joke.
I like readings better: I like words,
but I like hearing too — sometimes listening hurts.

Styx and the Stones can wound and hurt
with their volume and chords, and I get bored
listening to bands musicalize empty words
and render clichés rocked into song.
It's all one long unbroken rhythmic joke,
as if we, the audience, have all the time

in the world — yet we have no time.
I can say from experience it never hurts
to listen to a badly told joke
as long as you don't look bored.
It's like someone else's favorite song
you don't like: You learn the words

to make them happy, but alone the words
are actually pretty lame, especially times
when they're just sing sing singing that song —
but they really can't sing. You don't want to hurt
their feelings, but you *are* bored,
and inwardly laugh, thinking, "What a joke!"

Conversely, try telling your own joke.
Make up and write and rewrite your words
the next time you're at a reading, bored,
or are draped on the railing at a concert, killing time
you'll never get back, looking cool and hurt
and obviously so, like, over this song.

But if everyone is bored from just your telling the joke,
and you can't read music but you know the words,
you're wasting your time writing laughter — try hurt.

O Bury Me Not

I cannot escape the corn
nor walls for shadow rest

Red skies at night
when always always golden rays

The drivers laugh passing by
defeat in the wind
when we are winning

Fields whisper like cities shout
long nights wherever is home

Men permanently boys
shrugged into father coats
touch bombs before

dropping microcosms too
large to hold skin & ink

& corn gets put in everything
The dust explodes

Pick a season that's cruel
its pleasant memory
as landscape shields a strangled sob

The cut leaves growing space
repressed humanity needs to live
so one man can enjoy

the quality of light
upon such stricken ears
as Heaven conjures its own myth

of endlessness shattered
by a fence

Classic

Every film and cartoon I watched as a kid
too young to get into a theatre alone
was heavily edited for network television
The ceaseless blasting of Daffy Duck's face off
remained but the bull never exploded
The suicide bear only aired once that I saw

All the light T&A commercial broken
and cussing badly dubbed because
you couldn't say fuck and 6 other things
Sex was always off screen
Phoebe Cates out of the pool
never happened from the neck down
James Bond was merely salacious
like Pepe Le Pew
The girl in the after school special who had sex
for money learned a valuable lesson and went home
unlike rings busted on the news
Even *The Omen* on Sunday night
left the unavoidable train sandwich
to the imagination – frames excised
to fit the prime-time slot

Layers of mediated experience
flayed apart by letterboxed director's cuts
smearing screens in undiluted gore
when I thought I had seen it all

Taxi Driver 4pm on Saturday afternoon
minus the slow dance with her pimp
Apocalypse Now whittled down to 2.5 hours
Warner Bros. witch doctors with nose bones stayed
but enough violence cut
to make Bugs Bunny less cruel

My imagination was rated R
protected from the un-reality of art
while the news filled the margins
with a curated narrative and enough space
for a word from our sponsors

Our Solemn Debris

In the quiet of the evening of the end
with the sidewalks empty and traffic nonexistent
one by one neighbors wheel separate trash and
recycling totes to the curb automatically
trained and uniform as their gray and yellow bins

We are keeping it together one foot from the street and
at least four feet apart so tomorrow morning
the mechanical arm of the upgraded trucks
can grip with assurance and hoist
receptacles like whiskey shots

knocking back into a wet brown gob
compacted toasts for every human
the virus tucks away behind nuclear doors
inwardly thrashing with panic yet calm
enough to save reusables from a landfill fate

The Seashell & the Clergyman

He holds it to his ear
& hears the universe
speak his name

an orchestra
of clear reverence
& wizened listening

while I get static hiss
echo of my halting
tinnitus for reveries past

shhh they shush
shut up

a collection
of soaps in a basket
on the back of the toilet
in the bathroom at Mr Lubie

garbage truck backs up

garbage truck backs up
tuesday morning 6 AM
early chirping bird

Look Out Haskell It's Real

after Sooner or Later, *a documentary about the child star of* Medium Cool, *now a father 40 years later*

A part busted or missing
he definitely does not have plans to get it
Otherwise his motocross bike
is ready to go ready to win

Daddy showed him how to fix
Knew it knows engines intimately
but it hasn't run for a month
Tried to trick it out
Get a little more power
It's his and his problem now

Daddy spends an afternoon
Carving new pistol grips
with a knife sharpened so often
it looked like a marlin spike

Laughs when the cameraman says it
though he'd never heard "marlin" before
Son Haskell leans over on the couch
"As a big ol fish bout like at"

Daddy's eyes widen he nods
laughs laughs at everything
till Haskell says he's dropping out

"If I'd known then what I know
now I'd have stayed in" but why
hangs like hand-me-down shed tools
no one's touched in a generation
Not for any job needs doing

The camera catches fear
body language inarticulate
uncertainty of unwanted attention
Director hoped for redemption
an outpouring of regret
but Daddy has no words for his situation
introspection as alien as algebra

In '68 they scooped him up
out of Uptown Chicago
put him back after the shoot
like a tails-up penny

Appalachia reabsorbed him
coal seams and trees
now cleft by machine
"It don't matter" Haskell says
No argument there

Days move at the frame
rate of natural light
They had a nimble crew back then
navigating riot cops to get shots
Here the tripod is locked off
Waiting ages for something to happen
As bad as it is
it's worse elsewhere
or so they hear and repeat
to themselves neighbors kin

Laugh laugh until silence
Call it defense mechanism
He laughs at that too

All this waiting

cannot be good
but the clocks don't mind
their unreadable faces
and backs to the wall
Nothing ages you like
the death of your father
Man of the house now
Lord of La-Z-Boy Manor
We gave oxygen back
Ran out of boxes for pill
bottles syringes inhalers
O Library of Unread Cancer Books
Unlistened-To CDs on Breathing
Whey Requiring Decades and more
faith than Amazon ships free
speak of hope and broken promises
The kitchen clock needs winding
every eight days we keep
the key inside no warning
some middles of night
it simply stops

his crooked smile

his crooked smile
on the same side of my face
photos of my dad

Can you be still?

I only ask
I bequeath
the innocence of a star
to all remembering a name

Let us have more persevering ash
at cleansing ends
& speak it O and sing

Who among us staves off decay
is not worthy of aging well

Hearses proud resemble the plow
for knowing is also work
after we are resigned

The light does not go away
but where it remains
requires darkness of a kind

& kindness where the dead
have lost the will to speak

Common night heaven
full of light & touched
for believers

the rest dust

Injection site

We got a flag because
he'd been in the service
but had to order it
from the casket catalogue
Packing up his unused needles
like a dead soldier's locker
to ship home to Mom
waiting in the empty
house she's made over
carpets curtains darker woodwork stain
everything but his La-Z-Boy
I hear him sleeping in it now
needles bound for diabetics
in some other state
I learned too late to matter
I was not the kind of enemy
grunts defeat but
the adversarial construct
industries create to justify
martial law other big sticks
Dad fought unseen enemies
he took to the grave
I armed him with
a knife of his I stole
tucked away back in his casket
It's terrifying how
a family can change

in mere moments months
Styrofoam peanuts to protect
syringes and lancets all
a-hammering at his heart
as I discover what I can
get by without in this world
is of course addressed
to Gainesville, Florida
the length of time I spend
with his clothes and watch
before I wash off his DNA
and wear them every day
is my opt-out of acknowledgment
for my gift I claim
the shirts and jackets
recently smelled of him
tape down corrugated edges
these castoffs spare ammo
delivered to another empty weapon

Chain

We all hold hands in a circle
as if the weather were a thing we could deny.
Arrows at the edge of the target,
stray and quivering with failure.
You may not draw fire but this
circuit of co-conspirators is a lightning rod.
The tall grass beats itself into seeding.
There and everywhere the world breaks
a point in creation is divined, connected
by phantom root and silver air.
Thread notches our teeth in the end
after a lifetime of mended seams.
This all comes about willingly,
the only accident our arrangement:
boy girl boy girl.

Monster

How ever many times it happened then
or happens now inside your head

His shadow on your hide-away
scraggly pubic beard
blue-light teeth humming
a made-up bedtime tune

In journals your father
is hands and eyes
on flashlight paragraphs
around the scene of a crime

Frozen by his slathered spit
his singing to calm you down

The headboard not your friend
cold sheet shiver in
the hope he might be dead
He will always be inside
closer
inches away
closer
Here comes the monster
closer
Our love-proof fuck
closer

Me unfit for parenthood
closer

I get closer
coarse and why
you cannot make it stop

Every time we three are together

You frozen solid in my arms
He as useful as a candle
in a coffin full of gasoline
You stop
inside explode deep
Conversations bustle and roar around
the shadow across your face
in a room full of laughter you stop
We know where you are coming
for you tromping the forest primeval
to the doorstep of doll house or sepulcher

In a laundry list of fine details you rattle off
about what happened
you are the one
that obscures how this ends
A fractured procedural

you can never share and be safe
from the childhood monster
I conjure out of this

Morning Pages

Every time I type your name
it's different like forms of snow
that don't matter while shoveling

I can hear your punctuation
written out how to breathe
where to stop and start
over and over

A million notes without music
typed too fast transposing
letters & saying things wrong
edited later toward strange
meanings nattering at editors

I know who you are
grimmer & darker
negative easy when no one
tells you to frown
Make it till you break it
& burst like a distant star
gassy old brilliant

Walk through every open door
is advice I hear
unaware where I am going to
Who can parse a voice – you?

Every time I spell you out
a thing less useful conjured
slumps bidden to a threshold
while I explain how one
gets better writing
so as not to forget

ouroboros

Single torn-out leaf
Breaking signature math
Chewing fist crumpling
Last letter bolus
Enzymes digesting tongues

More could be said

But every word meal
Starving on foraged
Bits under nails
Defensive rent wounds
Making room for sawdust

A trophy atrophied

Warning a twig
Snapped and rustling
Notes scattered blowflies
Carcass stripped of us
Disappearing into wild

Jaws completely re-hinged

Secrets of Success

Hate equally.
Love discriminately.
Not everything is a nail
but anything can be used as a hammer.
Kill something and eat it.
Banish all fear from your core.
Let its refugees languish
at the border of your free zones.
Send aid reluctantly and gloat.

Stare off into space
but *see something*.
Say thank you and shut up.
This is the Time.
This is the Place.
You are the Person.
Learn to use a microphone.
Do the dishes. Do them.
When you come home late
to a bed made that morning
'tis as if someone cares.
Lifestyle not Life Support.
Love every award.
Forget they exist.
Whatever you are feeling
it is absolutely essential
that you feel and express it
and it is OK if everyone ignores you.

Indifference is a time-saver.
Even the Dalai Lama is neither vegan nor vegetarian.

Art is 99% frame.
Collaborate in spite of yourself.
Start everything immediately – be good later.
Be comfortable with the unknowable.
Say yes before you know.
Contrarians hate compulsively.
Develop your purpose.
Hoard but purge.
Being polite is the simplest way
to confound your detractors.
Grow where you are planted.
Dream but wake up.
Friends are a slippery slope.
Anything calls itself family what ain't blood
still hopes you will grow up and act right.
Make it funny, not fun.
Observe Experience Read Write Revise Edit Submit
Believe everything everyone says about you.
Ignore everything everyone says about you.
Liberate yourself from guilt.
Live life as both punishment and reward
you couldn't possibly deserve
but here goes.

The Social Safety Net

People recite the same prayer
every day many times a day
for most of their lives
because it beats repeating
the same old curse
but you still gotta keep one
on hand because who knows

Speech to the Aimless

worse than happening   waiting for dark
cheek to jowl   clashing in rain
watchful under apricot skies   near the taboo mark
unable to comfort   unwilling the pain

clashing in the rain   cheek to jowl
i ought to be shamed   animal cursing
unwilling the pain   unable to comfort
long on wondering   helpless nursing

animal cursing   i ought to be shamed
heaven a compartment   the grass grown long
helpless nursing   long on wondering
packed tight as a river   elemental song

the grass grown long   heaven a compartment
i say many things   fields full of bees
elemental song   packed tight as a river
in the middle lies the heart   blessed disease

fields full of bees   i say many things
near the taboo mark   watchful under apricot skies
blessed disease   in the middle lies the heart
waiting for dark   worse than happening

unputdownable

it is so important to be solitary and attentive when one is sad
... the seemingly uneventful and motionless moment
when our future steps into us is so much closer to life
than that other loud and accidental point of time
when it happens to us as if from outside
—Rilke, letter #8

Hey little one
This tendentious world
so much too much for you
keeps its place with bent pages
rough scraps of paper
backs of sticky-less post-it lists
postcard & handbill
occasional actual bookmark
memorial program
formal poem gift
No simple placeholder
but objet d'art itself
You were that too little one
part of our ongoing narrative
& marked a place
we now return to
The story needs
our eyes & sullen stern
thinking & memorized
innate love
to reach resolution

We flip to where we once pored
pick it right back up
Plot thread line word
come rushing back to us
neither beginning nor end
A new start

Apologies

Apologies these days come with a but
negating everything thereafter

I'm sorry but we needed wood
I'm sorry but humans trump birds
I'm sorry but it was on sale
I'm sorry but when you're older you'll understand

Confused birds don't wait
for the right kind of tree to grow
Telephone poles are native species
Even squirrel takes a quick look
& moves on – nuts

It's the emptiness of the promise fulfilled
that gets Nature Girl looking back
on a 50-yr movement morphed
into a wish for what coulda been

Bluebird does not think we're better
off in highly regarded cages
but he's in there hoping
not to be the canary
saving someone who doesn't even care

I'm sorry but she cares
Do you not see the antlers

filled with birds with no place
else to land?

She cares atop the dais of our making
One for everyone to step up to struggle
To speak for the trees
Sorry is nothing without action
& there it is as expected: but

Tooth and Nail

From the very beginning
there was nothing but noise
in and around machinery.

A brash oil smell.
Engines and the hum
of oxygenated carbon.

That's life outside a rubber
articulated into a weakness.
A meat sadness
presided over by a host of angels
who can shatter glass with bare hands
without cracking a smile.

The sun will not save us
trapped here in the spoiling
breadbox of the Earth.
In the end there is only silence

in this cavernous flesh and these still bones
hinting at a more calculated precision.
Fuel of a different sort.

For outer space. From inner space.
In quitting time and the slow-down.
Downsize. Layoff. Strike.

The halting rhythm of a cog
that has stopped
and now has time
to redefine its purpose.

Damn Broke

Back when the river flowed
I wrote all night to weather a flood
When it stopped it snowed
Mist over water and mud

I wrote all night to weather a flood
The cards turned in my favor
Mist over water and mud
Buried a human labor

The cards turned in my favor
Lost in nonsense scales
Buried a human labor
Mercy the sun entails

Lost in nonsense scales
Good work in better places
Mercy the sun entails
Making wild faces

Good work in better places
When it stopped it snowed
Making wild faces
Back when the river flowed

Blessed are the moneychangers for they bear sweet low-hanging fruit

His hand fell like an axe,
cleaving usurers' benches,
and shekels rang like chains unbound.
Where He scattered coins
lame beggars swarmed.

Incredulous lenders intervened
but apostle muscle held them back,
the LORD working miracle
after miracle of elbow, knee, fist.

Then lo, did a meager monger approach,
face bloodied, head bowed, garments rent,
saying: "P-please, dear GOD, my livelihood!
I'm up for junior partner next year!"

The messiah smote him mightily then
with the back of His hand, a ringing slap.
Yea, for even in the least of these
our savior compounds no interest.

Wolf Trap

The bar at Applebee's in Wolf Trap VA
is the saddest place in the universe
outside of a jammed airport in Kabul
I'm serious – people here are dead
No one has the decency to close their eyes

The tender leans over my notebook
"Dude writes like that – he's asking for it"
as if I'm going to get it
"They're going to label you" he says
oblivious to his own tag & flair

I've been dressing like an old man
since the 90s – it's all that shows
up at Goodwill: dead men's shoes

Suddenly on TV we have won
as if a bar fight left
behind in a bloody heap
makes one a champion
As if scoring in a parking lot
from a stranger at a concert
makes one crafty & cooler
than a stranger in an alley
As if the fightin' fix
did more than shim the banks

The tender rings the last call bell
I'm done but of course have another
Pavlovian response
in place of foreign policy

Some guys make bets squeezing
bar towels into a snifter
$5 – any takers?
There's always one &
if not there's one
out there on the verge
Maybe not $5 – maybe $10
or a smile from the right pretty face

Some nights they do it for nothin'
which is still something
but try telling that to a soldier on leave

Ten Million Dollar Halliburton Poem

You – holder holding me holding my stock
For the holders of shares who mean the world
with mean business – its targets & markets

We would salute thee were we true military
Instead let us dance 'cross the suq
under pale Arab moons – upon blood-red dunes
our grunts bust on on anxious sorties
plucking like ouds lost souls
repurposed for our brave new rendition
of a love song – a torch song for firing pallets
of greenbacks like stingers 'cross petro-black fields
tracer rounds straight to your heart
from KOЯN-blasting turrets
battering erectile adhan-drenched minarets

Don't fret lovelies – this pillow talk of war
where all is fair and love
is but negotiation as the soft target
of the white underbelly of your tru-tru passion
exposes where my conflict needs to go
hands-deep in each other's tactical pockets
muttering safe words no one will hear

The tender rings the last call bell
I'm done but of course have another
Pavlovian response
in place of foreign policy

Some guys make bets squeezing
bar towels into a snifter
$5 – any takers?
There's always one &
if not there's one
out there on the verge
Maybe not $5 – maybe $10
or a smile from the right pretty face

Some nights they do it for nothin'
which is still something
but try telling that to a soldier on leave

Ten Million Dollar Halliburton Poem

You – holder holding me holding my stock
For the holders of shares who mean the world
with mean business – its targets & markets

We would salute thee were we true military
Instead let us dance 'cross the suq
under pale Arab moons – upon blood-red dunes
our grunts bust on on anxious sorties
plucking like ouds lost souls
repurposed for our brave new rendition
of a love song – a torch song for firing pallets
of greenbacks like stingers 'cross petro-black fields
tracer rounds straight to your heart
from KOЯN-blasting turrets
battering erectile adhan-drenched minarets

Don't fret lovelies – this pillow talk of war
where all is fair and love
is but negotiation as the soft target
of the white underbelly of your tru-tru passion
exposes where my conflict needs to go
hands-deep in each other's tactical pockets
muttering safe words no one will hear

20th Anniversary

We'd not yet become brands
just people with untethered cameras
shooting footage only relatives
would see in e-picture frames
I use "we" collectively
though these were individual
decisions being made: go
shopping & save us from terror

There was no place to tell
how stupid this was unless
you were a newspaper
Veterans of the loudness war
happy wild & deaf

The name tags all read Mabel
perfectly poetic that way
& they're rude to you on purpose
Then everybody laughs
at the insolent help

Regardless of percentages
we rounded up the tip & called it good
Didn't care for the rich food
so here – learn a lesson in thrift
while we bomb back up
a mountain draped in flags

Every car looks presidential
& in a few years we'll be living
in the White House of our Dodge

Proud for what we endured
that day in Pigeon Forge & Gatlinburg
in October of 2001

Guidelines

Cemetery is the safest place
plots sharp as hospital corners
little stone poems
or children on them
and puppies and kittens
butterflies racecars pianos

not a death's head in sight

thank god for dates
and the ageless before the wars
statues with hats and guns
leading tombstone platoons

no one around but keepers
on their knees in daylight
blasting leaves around
fetching litter into buckets

tiny flags making tiny snaps
not even the joggers see

at Cousin Jeffrey's funeral
when we were 4
I went to find him
in the groundskeeper shed

nobody told me different
I disappear 'round a bend
past a shield of solitude
rising at the unclosing gates

Advice heard randomly do not take

There is a shortage of happiness
in the world we tend

toward austerity & desire &
tiny unfulfilled spaces lived in

a few decades & leave behind less
a statement than expression

Brief eye contact on trains
occurring amid dark costumes & bright

flashing windows many times
over the course of bland commutes

Love & lust the mind
plays out a dozen tryst scenarios

In some we marry grow old
our children hold our hands

as we pass one soon after the other
& stop pouring before the cup

overflows happy to have
something to drink

Our Origin

Tell me a story
not how your day has been
that you cleaned the cat box
took out the trash
after clearing the refrigerator
of dead uneaten food

House spirits care for these details
and the piles of spite is takes
to motivate your ass
to chore away a Saturday

I want your legends and myths
not the lie-consuming cycle
requiring a ladder to properly tuck away
or the rumor slouching down Main

Sirens going *whoop whoop*
through the intersection have it
cammed for their protection

Will we be stranded on this rock?
Forever? I remember how to make a raft
from a movie and the movie
in my head where Dad was there
to tell me how and do it all himself

Where fate got slammed a pool formed
I filled it with neat colored rocks
I found along the riverbank

Not naturally occurring
A plot – some action and a truth

The eyes glaze over because telling
is no substitute for a show
reduced in this textual world
to merely unbelievably enthralling

Back into the stars you go
Up up into the cloud
with ringing ears
from the chorus glory

Nothing need be foretold
but save us from the random
with singular vision
and undeniable breath

Leave nothing out
and make it good

Tony Brewer has lived in Indiana forever. He has performed coast to coast and recorded for community and public radio as well as NPR Playhouse and the HEAR Now Audio Fiction & Arts Festival. His books include *Hot Type Cold Read* (Chatter House Press, 2013), *Homunculus* (Dos Madres Press, 2019), *The History of Projectiles* (Alien Buddha Press, 2021), and *Tabletop Anxieties & Sweet Decay* (with Tim Heerdink, Roaring Junior Press, 2021). He frequently collaborates with experimental audio collective Urban Deer Recording Cvlt and is one-third of the poetry performance group Reservoir Dogwoods.

More at tonybrewer71.blogspot.com.

www.ingramcontent.com/pod-product-compliance
Lightning Source LLC
Chambersburg PA
CBHW030337100526
44592CB00010B/720